Dedicated To:
St. James Academy
High School

Written By: Abigail Gartland

Hello, my name is St. James!

This is my brother, John. We were both apostles of Jesus!

My brother, John, and I would spend our days fishing.

One day, while we were out fishing, we met a man named Jesus.

He asked us to follow Him, and we did!

We went on so many adventures with Him, and became his apostles.

There were two apostles named James. I was known as James the Greater, and the other one was known as James the Lesser.

I was one of Jesus' favored followers. I was honored to witness many of His miracles that the other apostles didn't get to see.

One day, Jesus was approached by a man named Jairus. He said that his young daughter had passed away.

We followed the man to his house where we found the young girl passed away in her bed.

Everyone was so sad, but Jesus said that she was not dead; she was just sleeping.

We were very confused, but Jesus put His head down and prayed. He said, "Little girl, arise."

Suddenly, the little girl opened her eyes and sat up.

Jesus performed a miracle and brought her back to life!

We saw many miracles during the life of Jesus.

After Jesus died, I traveled all the way to Spain to share His teachings with people.

Do you want to be more like me?

You can celebrate my feast day with me on July 25th.

I am the patron saint of blacksmiths and Spain.

I pray for you every day of your life.

St. James Pray for us!

Copyright:

Clipart:  © LimeandKiwiDesigns
Licensed purchased: 1/10/2024

About the Author

Abigail Gartland

I love the saints and I love my faith. The idea for sharing the stories of the saints with little ones came when my dear friends were expecting their first baby. I wanted to create something as unique and special as our friendship. Each book is dedicated to very special people and groups who have enriched my faith in different ways. I am blessed to write these stories and appreciate the unending support of my family and friends. When I am not writing, I am a middle school teacher. I hope you enjoy these stories. I pray for each and every person who opens one of my books to learn more about the saints.

Abbie

www.ingramcontent.com/pod-product-compliance
Lightning Source LLC
LaVergne TN
LVHW051042070526
838201LV00067B/4889